Science Matters
WHEELS AND AXLES

Erinn Banting

WEIGL PUBLISHERS INC.

Published by Weigl Publishers Inc.
350 5th Avenue, Suite 3304, PMB 6G
New York, NY USA 10118-0069
Website: www.weigl.com

Library of Congress Cataloging-in-Publication Data

Library of Congress Cataloging-in-Publication Data available upon request.
Fax 1-866-44-WEIGL for the attention of the Publishing Records department.

ISBN 978-1-60596-033-3 (hard cover)
ISBN 978-1-60596-034-0 (soft cover)

Printed in China
1 2 3 4 5 6 7 8 9 13 12 11 10 09

Editor Nick Winnick
Design and Layout Terry Paulhus

Photograph Credits

Weigl acknowledges Getty Images as its primary image supplier for this title.

Contents

What is a Wheel?

Wheels and axles can be found all around you. When people drive a car, ride a Ferris wheel, or roll on a skateboard, they are using wheels and axles. Wheels even help go-karts roll down streets and tracks.

A wheel is a circle-shaped object that rotates around its center. Wheels often have an axle in the middle to hold them in place while they rotate.

■ Wheels and axles together are one of six simple machines. People use simple machines to make daily tasks easier.

How do Wheels Help?

Wheels make it easier to carry heavy objects over long distances.

Wheels turn in a circle, or rotate. If the round edge of a wheel is resting on a surface when it turns, the wheel will move forward.

Wheels were first used to carry objects in carts and wagons. Over time, many other uses for wheels were discovered, such as grinding grain and telling the time.

Wheels in Time

The earliest forms of transportation did not have axles or wheels. This made moving people or heavy loads from place to place very difficult. Most people traveled on foot or on horses. Goods or building materials had to be carried or dragged along the ground.

Dragging an object across a surface creates **friction**. Friction makes it difficult for one surface to slide against another. The rougher the surfaces, the more friction there will be between them.

■ Many early drawings show wheels and how they were used long ago.

How did Wheels Help?

When wheels were invented, moving heavy objects from place to place became much easier.

Early humans realized that to move things more easily, they needed to reduce friction. Rollers were made by placing a number of logs on the ground side by side. The material being transported was laid on top of the logs. When the load was pulled, the logs rolled, and the load moved forward.

Rollers reduced friction, but people still looked for a way to move heavy objects using less **force**. According to some **archaeologists**, wooden wheels were developed as early as 8000 BC. Wheels reduce friction, so objects sitting on wheels can be moved the same distance with much less force.

What is an Axle?

Wheels on their own are useful, but they have many more uses when combined with axles. An axle is a straight rod connected to the center of a wheel. The difference in size between the wheel and the axle is what makes a wheel system more useful than a simple roller.

The greater distance the wheel turns, the more force is applied to the axle. In the same way, the more force that is applied to the axle, the greater distance the wheel will turn.

■ Spokes make a wheel very strong, but much lighter, than a solid wheel.

Putting it All Together

Wheels and axles work together in two ways.

Some wheels and axles are attached. As the wheel turns, the axle turns as well. When the wheel is turned, the axle produces more force than was used to turn the wheel. This is because the outer edge of the axle moves much less distance than the outer edge of the wheel. What the axle saves in distance, it makes up for in force. Doorknobs are an example of this kind of wheel and axle. A rod, or axle, is attached to the knob, or wheel. Turning the rod latches and unlatches the door. However, it is difficult to turn the rod on its own. The knob is used to turn the rod more easily.

Other wheels turn around an axle. In these cases, it is usually the axles that drive the wheels forward. A greater force must be applied to the axle, but the wheel moves with more speed. This is how cars and bicycles work. Force is applied to the axles, which turn the wheels.

Rolling Forward

Wheels and axles have changed over time. From rollers to heavy wooden wheels, people keep looking for ways to improve the simple machine.

As **technology** improved, many changes were made to wheels. Over time, people made wheels and axles in different shapes and sizes. A variety of different materials were used to build them, and they were used for different purposes. Wheels have become so important to daily tasks that they can be found in everything from watches to spacecraft.

■ Aircraft, such as space shuttles, use wheels for takeoff and landing.

Important Inventions

Here are a few important inventions that improved wheels and axles.

Spoked Wheels

Spokes are rods that connect the center of a wheel to the edge, or rim. They can be used instead of solid wheels to make the whole wheel lighter. The first wheels with spokes were built 4,000 years ago in parts of Europe and Asia.

Chariots

Around 2000 BC, people began to use chariots. A chariot is a light cart with two wheels that is pulled by a horse. The design of chariots was later **adapted** to make carts and carriages.

Tires

In the early 1900s, the first cars were built and sold. Rubber tires helped the wheels of these early cars to grip the ground and move more safely.

Modern Wheels

The wheel and axle is a simple machine, but in today's world, it is rarely used on its own. Instead, wheels are often found as part of a complex machine.

Complex machines are combinations of many different simple machines that work together to do a task. Cars, bicycles, and boats are all examples of complex machines that use wheels.

■ One of the best known uses for wheels and axles is on a car.

Wheels and Axles at Work

Wheels and axles are found in many common machines.

Trains

Trains have straight axles. A straight axle is a long rod with a wheel connected to each end. Straight axles are very useful for trains because they can support a great deal of weight.

Cars

Cars and trucks use split axles. Each wheel is attached to a separate shaft. This lets the wheels turn at slightly different speeds. This helps cars and trucks turn more quickly.

Music and Movies

An axle holds the disc in place inside a DVD or CD player. The axle spins the disc so the machine can read it. Turning the disc from the center keeps it from shaking and skipping.

A Wheel With Teeth

A gear is a wheel with teeth around the edge. The teeth are short spikes that mesh up with spikes on other gears, like the teeth on a zipper.

Gears are useful because, when the teeth from one gear mesh with another, turning one gear will turn the other. These special wheels are very useful in many machines, from watches to motor vehicles.

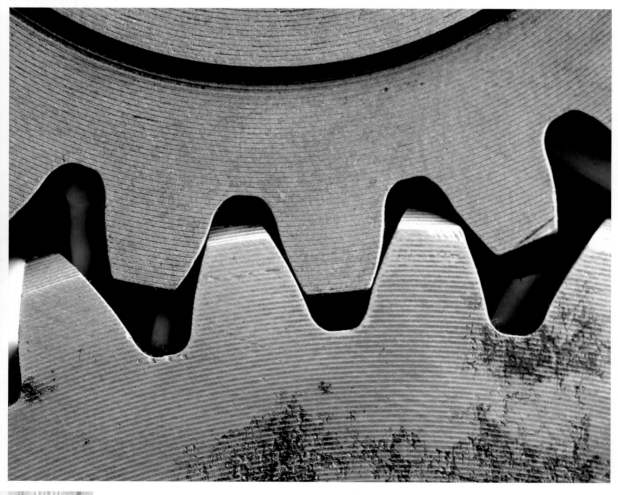

■ The teeth of a set of gears need to match perfectly, or they will wear and break down.

Changing Gears

Gears are most useful when combined with other gears of different sizes. Depending on the size of the gears used, the force and speed of the turning gears can be changed.

Large gears are easy to turn but need to be turned very fast to push an object, such as a car or bike, forward. Smaller gears need more force to be turned, but can move an object forward faster.

A great deal of force is needed to start the vehicle moving in a small gear. For this reason, large gears are used when a vehicle first starts moving.

The engine must turn a large gear very fast to move at a high speed. Once a vehicle has built up speed, a larger gear can be shifted to a smaller one.

The Future of Wheels

Every day, **engineers** research and design new ways to travel and make life better. As machines change, so do the way people use wheels and axles.

The cars on roads today have four wheels and two axles. This might change in the near future. Some car manufacturers are looking for ways to make smaller cars. These cars may only have two or three wheels. They take up less space and use less fuel.

Electronics can be used in many places where wheels were once needed. The gears of a watch can be replaced by special crystals. Early calculators used moving parts, such as wheels. Now, these parts can be replaced with **microchips**. This saves a great deal of space and **energy**.

■ Some concept cars have the ability to "lean" while turning. This makes them more stable.

A Life of Science

George Ferris

George Ferris was born in 1859 in Galesburg, Illinois. After university, he worked as an engineer, designing bridges. Ferris used his knowledge of science and simple machines to design one of the largest wheels in the world. His idea was inspired by the wheel of a bicycle. He called it an "observation wheel," but the design soon came to be known as a Ferris wheel.

The first Ferris wheel was built in 1893. Since then, thousands of Ferris wheels have been built around the world.

One of the largest Ferris wheels in the world is the London Eye in London, England. The London Eye lets riders view the city from 443 feet (135 meters) in the air.

Gaining an Advantage

There are six simple machines. They are *inclined planes*, *levers*, *pulleys*, *screws*, *wedges*, and the *wheel and axle*. All simple machines are designed to make work easier. These machines do not have batteries or motors. They do not add any energy of their own to help people do work. So, how do simple machines work?

Simple machines work by changing the forces that are applied to them. In most cases, they do this by changing the distance or direction of a force.

Inclined Planes

Inclined planes are sloping surfaces that connect a lower level to a higher level or the opposite.

Lever

A lever is a moveable bar that rests on a solid point called the fulcrum.

Pulley

A pulley is a wheel with a groove around the outside edge. In this groove, there is a rope or cable. Pulling the rope turns the wheel.

Screw

Screws are tube-shaped tools with sharp edges spiralling around them. They are often used to fasten objects together.

Wedge

A wedge is a triangle-shaped tool with a sharp edge. It can separate two objects, lift an object, or hold an object in place.

Wheel and Axle

Wheels are circle-shaped objects that rotate around their center. They often have an axle in the middle to hold them in place.

Surfing Simple Machines

How can I find more information about simple machines?

- Libraries have many interesting books about simple machines.
- Science centers have good information on how simple machines work.
- The Internet has many interesting websites about simple machines.

Where can I find a good reference website to learn more about wheels and axles?

Encarta Homepage
www.encarta.com

- Type any term related to simple machines into the search engine. Some terms to try include "wheel and axle" and "mechanical advantage."

Science in Action

Roll With It

Design your own car by building a simple machine.

You will need:

- a ruler
- a wooden skewer
- 2 washers
- plasticine
- 2 blank CDs

1. With the help of an adult, find two blank CDs.
2. Place the washers into the center of the CDs.
3. Place plasticine in the center of the washers.
4. Stick the skewer through the center of each wheel.
5. Roll your axle and wheels across the table or floor.

What Have You Learned?

1 What is a wheel?

2 What is an axle?

3 How is friction created?

4 What are spokes?

5 How many types of simple machines are there?

6 What is a gear?

7 What is the London Eye?

8 What were early calculators called?

9 When were the first wooden wheels made?

10 How many wheels and axles do most cars have?

Answers: 1. A wheel is a circle-shaped object that rotates around its center. **2.** An axle is a straight rod connected to the center of the wheel. **3.** Friction is created when one surface rubs against another. **4.** Spokes are rods that connect the center of a wheel to the edge, or rim. **5.** There are six types of simple machines. **6.** A gear is a wheel with teeth around the edge. **7.** The London Eye is one of the largest Ferris wheels in the world. It is located in London, England. **8.** Early calculators were called difference engines. **9.** Wooden wheels were developed as early as 8000 BC. **10.** Most cars have four wheels and two axles.

Words to Know

adapted: changed over time

archaeologists: scientists that study the past

electronics: circuits or devices

energy: power needed to do work

engineers: people who use science to solve practical problems

force: the push or pull needed to move something

friction: the force caused by two things rubbing against one another

microchips: small objects that can be used to make calculations

technology: devices or tools created to perform tasks

Index